NATIONAL
GEOGRAPHIC
KiDS

EVERYTHING ROBOTICS

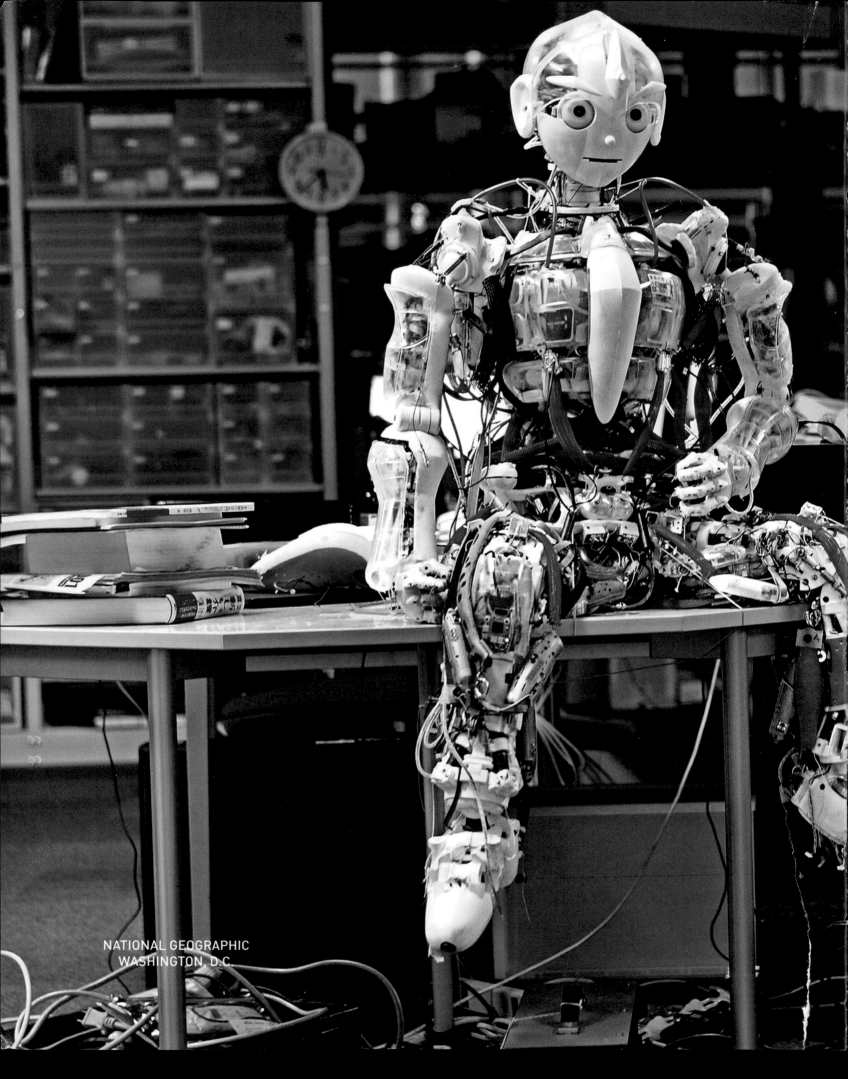

EVERYTHING
ROBOTICS

JENNIFER SWANSON

With National Geographic Explorer SHAH SELBE

CONTENTS

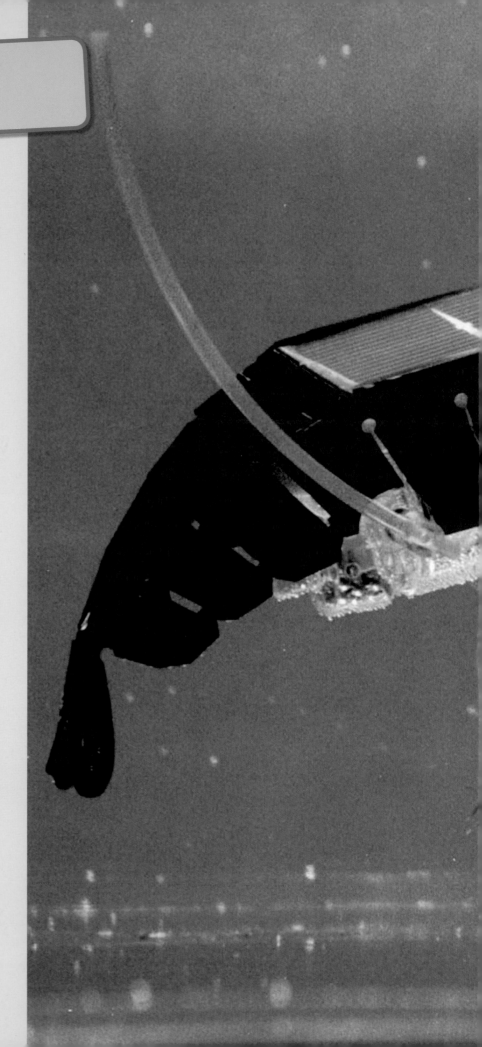

These Japanese robotic shrimp and crab toys are made to swim. They are powered by solar battery packs on their backs.

Robotic arms work on an automotive plant assembly line. Many automotive plant robots work alongside humans.

INTRODUCTION

ROBOTS. ARE THEY MACHINES
AND LIFELIKE AUTOMATONS THAT HELP

humans with their everyday tasks? Or are they mechanical beings that want to take over the world? Since we aren't talking about science fiction in a book or movie, most experts agree they are the former. Robots are, after all, human creations. They are the work of roboticists—scientists who combine engineering with computer science. The robots people deal with on a daily basis are helpful. They build things, catch criminals, explore the world, and fight wars. Robots also work in the home—vacuuming and cleaning. There are even robot nurses to care for you when you are sick, and robots that perform surgery.

What do robots look like? Some look like massive mechanical arms, and some like tiny flying bees. Many are designed to look like humans. We tend to feel more comfortable with designs that look like us. From businesses to police, and from our homes to outer space, robotic technology is created to serve humans and keep us safe, healthy, and informed about the world. So get ready to enter the world of cool and complex machinery and learn EVERYTHING about robotics!

EXPLORER'S CORNER

Hi! I'm Shah Selbe.

I am an engineer and conservation technologist, which basically means I develop technologies that can help us protect the environment and its wild animals. For the past ten years, I've created robotic technologies that have been used in space, throughout our oceans, and in nature reserves all over the world! My work takes engineering out of the lab and into the wild. Look for me throughout the book in the Explorer's Corners, where I will be sharing some of the amazing ways robots can save our planet! Come join me on a robotics adventure!

These robot windup toys are designed to look like machines with humanlike eyes, noses, mouths, and ears on their faces.

1

ROBOTS
RULE!

WHAT IS ROBOTICS?

ROBOTICS IS THE SCIENCE THAT DEALS WITH THE DESIGN, CONSTRUCTION, OPERATION,

and use of robots. Robots are machines that compute (or "think"), act, and sense the world around them.

ROBOTS AND ROBOTICS

Robots and robotics go hand in hand. Roboticists, or robot scientists, design, build, and test robots. A roboticist has imagined what a robot can do before that robot ever walks the earth, or is installed to do work in a factory, or is sent off to explore space. Robotics uses the science of engineering and computer programming to create machines that do things for humans. And robots do a lot of things. There are millions and millions of robots doing all kinds of work all over the world. Robots come in many shapes and sizes. There are robots with just one arm that make and assemble cars, pack boxes, and even release and retrieve satellites in space. These robots are usually managed by a human controller. But many robots are autonomous, meaning they are programmed to do tasks on their own.

QRIO

In the movie *Star Wars*, robot R2-D2 may have had a weird beeping language, but Luke Skywalker could still understand him.

QRIO is a dancing robot with voice recognition software that allows it to recognize human voices.

R2-D2

THINKING THINGS THROUGH

Most robots have a "brain." The brain is the technology center of the robot and is where all of the robots' "thinking" systems are found. The ASIMO robot, short for Advanced Step in Innovative Mobility, can walk, talk, and jump. It can do this because it has voice- and visual-recognition capabilities. That means it could identify you by your voice and image. These abilities allow ASIMO to communicate with us. Communication is key. We like to think of robots as interactive beings, similar to robots we see in movies.

BOT BITS MORE THAN 90 PERCENT OF THE WORLD'S ROBOTS WORK IN FACTORIES MAKING PRODUCTS.

ROBOTIC BRAINS

A robot brain is made up of tiny electronic parts called microcontrollers. Microcontrollers are commonly called microchips. A microchip is basically a computer that is shrunk down to a very tiny size. The microcontroller handles memory, input/output lines, and a central processing unit (CPU)—all the parts of a standard-size computer. It uses these parts to process the information it receives from the sensors. As with any other computer, the microcontroller can upload, store, and run a program. A human programmer creates a program for each robot brain. The program tells the robot what to do, how to act, and how to move.

A human operator works a robotic movie camera.

SENSING THE ENVIRONMENT

Some robots have sensors inside their microcontrollers. The sensors allow the robot to gather information about the environment in the same way our brain gathers information from our senses. The information from the sensors is processed in the CPU, and the robot reacts in the way it has been programmed to react. For example, if a robot senses an object in its path, the CPU might direct the robot to move around the object.

WHAT IS NOT A ROBOT?

You know your refrigerator is a machine that keeps your food cold, but is your refrigerator a robot? There isn't one ultimate definition of a robot, but experts agree that robots have some things in common. Robots move around, sense their environment, use at least one mechanical limb, and follow simple or complex programming. So, even though your fridge does have a thermometer that senses and adjusts the temperature, and a compressor that acts to keep your food cool, it doesn't move, pick things up, or talk to you. If your fridge isn't guided by a computer program and it doesn't have mechanical limbs, it is not a robot. But that doesn't mean that the fridge of the future couldn't be designed and programmed to walk around delivering cold drinks.

HRP-2

HRP-2 is sensing its surroundings and using its programming to balance and walk on a board.

AGE OF ROBOTS

ASIMO

IT MAY BE HARD TO BELIEVE, BUT
ROBOTS HAVE ONLY BEEN AROUND FOR LESS THAN
100 years. The idea of a robot, though, is practically prehistoric. The ancient Greeks had ideas for simple automatons, or humanlike robots, to help with daily tasks. But they would be amazed by what the robots of today can do!

IT TAKES TIME TO MAKE A ROBOT

Thinking machines have fascinated and frightened us for centuries. Why are we so determined to create a robot that walks, talks, and acts just like us? That's easy! We want to have something that imitates us and can do the jobs we do. The hard part is actually doing that. Constructing a humanoid robot is a staggering task. It takes years and years of research, trial and error, and many, many mistakes to get it right. The Honda Motor Company took almost 30 years to develop the ASIMO robot of today. A lot of the advances in robotics technology, such as walking and jumping, have happened in the last 5 years. Why does it take so long? Robotics technology, even of a basic robot arm, is complex. For a single robot arm, an engineer must create a shoulder, elbow, wrist, and sometimes a hand with fingers. Each of these parts must be programmed to move forward, backward, and twist in just the right direction. This gives the robot the ability to move up, down, left, right, forward, backward, and diagonally. Every movement requires a different command.

I, ROBOT

Science fiction author Isaac Asimov (1920–1992) wrote more than 500 books and short stories, many of which involve robots. In his book *I, Robot* (1950), he developed rules for how robots should interact with humans. These rules are known as the three laws of robotics, or Asimov's laws. The laws are a work of fiction, but they make us think about how machines should serve humans. The laws state that:

1. **ROBOTS MUST NOT INJURE OR HARM A HUMAN BEING.**

2. **ROBOTS MUST OBEY A HUMAN BEING, EXCEPT WHERE SUCH ORDERS WOULD CONFLICT WITH LAW #1.**

3. **A ROBOT MUST PROTECT ITSELF AS LONG AS THIS DOESN'T CONFLICT WITH LAW #1 OR LAW #2.**

ISAAC ASIMOV

ROBOTICS EVOLUTION

ELEKTRO AND SPARKO

BEST KNOWN FOR:
WALKING UNDER VOICE COMMAND

Elektro and Sparko were robots built by Westinghouse Electric between 1937 and 1939. They appeared as amazing wonders at the 1939 New York World's Fair. Elektro worked via 48 electrical relays. It could follow voice commands to walk and blow up balloons by voice command.

AUTOMATON

ELEKTRO AND SPARKO

ARTIST'S DEPICTION OF DNA NANOBOTS

AUTOMATONS

Automatons are self-operating machines, such as this musical automaton from the 1700s. Automatons are not robots, but they are early prototypes of machines that seem to act on their own.

DANTE II

BEST KNOWN FOR:
IDENTIFYING AND FIGHTING CANCER

Combining nanotechnology—the science of engineering really small things—with robotics programming, scientists are developing nanomachines that can deliver drugs to cancer cells. The nanomachines are built from DNA—the stuff that tells cells in the human body what to do. DNA nanobots are being tested to treat leukemia.

HRP SERIES

BEST KNOWN FOR:
HUMANOID ROBOTS THAT LOOK REALISTIC

The HRP series robots are designed to be domestic helpers—in other words, robot servants. They are known for their ability to stand up after lying flat, an achievement that took years of robotics research. The HRP-4C has a humanlike head and a voicebank that allows it to speak.

HRP-4C

DANTE II

BEST KNOWN FOR:
EXPLORING VOLCANOES

Dante II looks like a mechanical spider. With eight legs, it is no wonder why. This tethered, walking volcanologist robot was made to take samples from volcanoes where dangerous gases could kill human volcano researchers. Dante helps researchers explore and conduct experiments from a safe distance.

BOT BITS THE WORD "ROBOT" COMES FROM THE CZECH WORD *ROBOTA*, MEANING "FORCED LABOR."

ULTIMATE ROBOT FEATS

FROM PLAYING SOCCER TO DEFUSING
BOMBS TO STANDING IN FOR THE LOCAL DOCTOR, THESE BOTS
are tops. These mechanical marvels deserve awards for their amazing actions.

ROBO-ATHLETE OF THE YEAR

It kicks, it shoots, it scores! NAO, a robot produced by Aldebaran Robotics, can walk by itself, maneuver over different types of surfaces, and even play soccer. But NAO is not just athletically talented. It can also track and recognize faces, move out of the way of objects it encounters, and even listen and respond to you.

NAO

ROBO-BEST FRIEND

AlphaDog is one tough "pack" animal. AlphaDog is designed to look like a real dog. Well, sort of. With the ability to walk up steep mountains and down rocky trails, this dog is a welcome part of any soldier's kit. It can carry up to 400 pounds (181 kg) and walk 20 miles (32 km) in one day.

ALPHADOG

ROBO-RESCUER

Hello? Anyone out there? Not in your wildest nightmares would you imagine seeing a robot snake come at you. But if you are trapped in a building, that snake might just be your best friend. Researchers at Carnegie Mellon University, in Pennsylvania, U.S.A., have developed a robot snake that can slither into places humans and even rescue dogs can't get to. It mimics the movement of a real snake, which allows it to curve and bend into tight spaces. The snakebot has a camera so that the human controller can see where it's going.

SNAKEBOT

THE REAL ROBO-COP

TEODOR

Timing is everything. When seconds count, and a bomb might go off, this expert robot is called in. The tEODor robot created by Cobham has one mission: to defuse a bomb. Its one arm can delicately maneuver tiny wires and pieces of metal. The double-tread track keeps everything stable, while the camera allows the human controller to see up close without being within the blast range.

ROBO-DOC

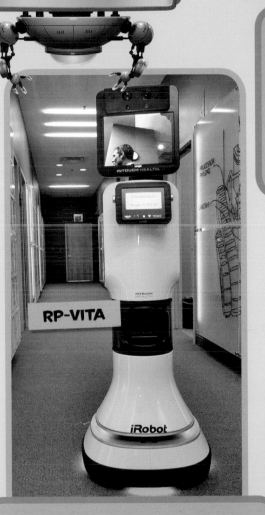

RP-VITA

Stick out your tongue and say *ahh*. This robot is standing in for the local doctor. It's called the Remote Presence Virtual + Independent Telemedicine Assistant, or RP-VITA for short. RP-VITA can't do anything major such as surgery or any kind of procedure, but it can monitor patients before and after surgery. This gives medical staff up-to-date information on patients when they might not be able to check on them in person.

NIMBLE DANCER

This bot has got the moves! HRP-4C is a humanoid robot designed to look like a real woman. It has a realistic body shape and face, and it responds to voice recognition. The coolest thing is that it can dance and sing! Its voice is a bit metallic, but it blends nicely with other singers.

HRP-4C

BOT BITS ALPHADOG CAN PLAY FETCH—WITH ITSELF.

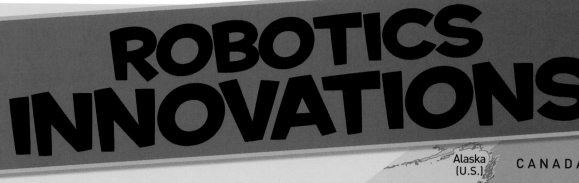

ROBOTICS INNOVATIONS

ROBOTS SWIM, SKI, AND FLY. SOME PLAY A MEAN GAME OF

table tennis. All over the world, robots are helping and challenging humans in a variety of endeavors.

Alaska (U.S.)

CANADA

NORTH

AMERICA

UNITED STATES

CANADA

Built at the University of Manitoba and standing just under 2 feet (0.6 m) tall, Jennifer the robot can skate, shoot, and score with the best of them. Outfitted with a tiny hockey stick and, of course, a helmet, Jennifer would be a great asset to any team. Jennifer also skis downhill and cross-country.

JENNIFER

U.S.A.

Researchers at Boston Dynamics have created a robot cheetah that can run almost half as fast as a real cheetah. A real cheetah runs about 70–75 miles an hour (112–120 km/h), but the robot cheetah can run 29 miles an hour (47 km/h) or more. Its speed and agility are helpful to humans because it can cover ground quickly and also carry packs of supplies for military or police use.

EXPLORER'S CORNER

Some of the most exciting work in robotics right now is being done with flying robots. There has been so much innovation in drone technology that it is becoming a major tool for how we collect scientific data about plants and animals to better protect the planet. Hobbyist engineers are now building drones that can fly hundreds of miles and stay in the air for hours at a time.

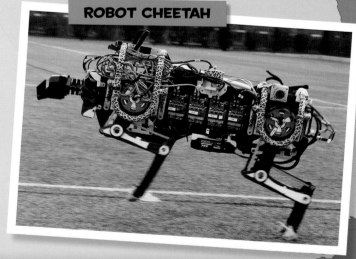

ROBOT CHEETAH

SOUTH AMERICA

ANTARCTICA

BOT BITS
CRABSTER IS A CAR-SIZE ROBOT DESIGNED IN KOREA FOR DEEP OCEAN RESEARCH.

UNITED KINGDOM

Britain launched the largest group of marine research robot boats ever launched at one time. The group included aquatic drones of all kinds, including the AutoNaut, a canoe-like robot with an antenna on top to collect information; and C-Enduro, an airboat that records water and weather data. The goal is to map the Atlantic Ocean floor, investigate local marine life, and gather information about the weather and climate in the area.

UNITED KINGDOM

EUROPE

ASIA

AFRICA

CHINA

JAPAN

EQUATOR

0 — 2,000 miles

0 — 2,000 kilometers

Robot drones are not new, but the type of visual input the BeeRotor receives is new. Its visual input is based on a winged insect, such as a butterfly or a moth. Unlike other drones, which rely on an accelerometer—a sensor that sweeps the ground back and forth to determine where it is—the BeeRotor uses the optic flow approach. Optic flow is what insects use to figure out their distance and speed as they fly.

C-ENDURO

The Henn-na Hotel in Nagasaki, Japan, is the first robot-staffed hotel. Its humanoid robot employees work at the front desk, checking human guests into the 72-room hotel. There are also robot porters, coat checkers, and housekeeping staff. There are some human employees, but over time the hotel expects to have robots make up 90 percent of its staff.

CHINA

World-famous table tennis player Timo Boll played against the "fastest Ping-Pong-playing robot in the world"—the KUKA KR Agilus robot. The robot was created by KUKA Robotics, one of the leading manufacturers of robots in the world. The match was held in China and recorded on video. While the play was intense, Boll ultimately won 11–9.

FUJITSU

AN ILLUSTRATED DIAGRAM

ROBONAUT 2

A ROBONAUT IS
A ROBOT DESIGNED TO
work directly with astronauts in space—sort of an astronaut's best friend. Robonaut 2 (R2) is a humanoid robot with better dexterity than the robotic systems usually used in space. In a confined area, it's a great advantage to have an extra pair of hands, eyes, and even legs that can grip things. And when that place is the International Space Station, it's even more handy because you can't just call up a neighbor for help. Let's take a closer peek inside what makes the extra-special Robonaut 2 an out-of-this-world assistant.

EYES
R2's eyes are four cameras behind the visor. Two of the cameras are for stereovision (seeing in 3-D) and two are auxiliary cameras.

HEAD
R2's head is designed to look like a human. The brain is not located here, though.

MOUTH
R2's mouth has an infrared camera to see in the dark.

HANDS
R2's hands can open, close, and grasp things with 5 pounds (2.2 kg) of force in each finger.

STOMACH
The control system, or brain, is located here. R2 has its own preprogrammed artificial intelligence so it can function autonomously or be controlled remotely by a human user.

BACKPACK

The power source, located in the backpack, can either be plugged in or can hold batteries.

ARMS

R2's arms can rotate for freedom of movement and hold up to 20 pounds (9 kg).

SPECS:

Materials:
Primarily aluminum with steel, and nonmetallics

Weight: 330 pounds (150 kg)

Height:
3 feet 4 inches (1 m) from waist to head
Legs add 4 feet 8 inches (1.4 m) to height

Shoulder width:
2 feet 7 inches (0.8 m)

Sensors. More than 350

Processors:
38 PowerPC processors

Speed:
Up to 7 feet (2.1 m) per second

SENSORS

Sensors are located in all of R2's appendages (hands, feet, head). They give R2 the ability to see and touch, just like a human.

LEGS

The legs allow R2 to be mobile. Each leg has tiny end effectors that act like toes and can bend and grip to move R2 around inside the station. The effectors can also be used outside if R2 needs to go for a space walk.

The German-designed Artificial Intelligence Lightweight Android, or AILA, presses switches on a computer panel. AILA was programmed to recognize the switches and to know how much force to apply when touching them.

ARTIFICIAL LIFE

ROBOT HISTORY

THE ANCESTORS OF TODAY'S ROBOTS HAVE BEEN AROUND FOR CENTURIES.

They weren't like the robots of today, of course. They couldn't walk or talk. In fact, these early machines were more like mechanical toys.

AUTOMATON

Automatons are mechanical toys and oddities.

AUTOMATONS

The ancient Greeks had automatons, or self-operating machines. Automatons mimicked human or animal actions. They had mechanical parts that sometimes required a person to push or turn a lever. By the 1700s, some automatons were sophisticated enough to play music. Some automatons served tea, and some were made to act like real animals. A duck automaton made in France in 1739 could flap its wings, drink water, and eat grain and then "poop" it out.

Mr. ROBOT THE MECHANICAL BRAIN

★ Watch lights go on and off while he walks.
★ Operates on flashlight batteries.
★ Make him walk by winding up spring mechanism.

PAT. 30-3023   PAT. 30-11313

ROBOTICS TIME LINE

1495
Leonardo da Vinci draws the first humanoid robot knight.

1801
French weaver Joseph-Marie Jacquard makes a mechanical loom that uses perforated cards for stringing cloth, the Jacquard loom influenced early computer designs.

1822
English mathematician and engineer Charles Babbage proposes the difference engine—a mechanical calculator that paved the way for later computers.

1843
Ada Lovelace translates a French paper on Charles Babbage's analytical engine and adds her ideas; she is later referred to as the first computer programmer.

1921
Czech writer Karel Čapek first uses the word "robot" in his 1921 play *R.U.R. (Rossum's Universal Robots)* to describe a group of workers created to toil for humans.

1937–39
Elektro, the first humanoid robot that can walk and talk, is created by Westinghouse.

German-made AILA, or Artificial Intelligence Lightweight Android, gently shakes a human hand.

ARTIFICIAL INTELLIGENCE

The science of robotics combines computers with engineering. Modern robots are machines with electrical parts that have computer programming. A robot's programming allows or directs it to do things. Early automatons were just mechanical, but many of today's robots and robotic systems have artificial intelligence, or AI. AI is a computer system that can perform tasks that require humanlike intelligence or reasoning. These include seeing objects, recognizing speech, and making decisions.

GO, SHAKEY, GO!

With a name like Shakey, you might not expect much, but the world's first robot to use AI was a major step in robot history. Shakey was named for its characteristic rough movement. But it was the first robot that could "think." In other words, Shakey could follow a command, "see" its surroundings, and plan a route to move around objects. After Shakey, robotics engineers set about mimicking how animals and humans behave. Their goal was to make a robot that could walk, talk, run, jump, and function just like a human.

TROODY

The first robotic dinosaur, modeled after a *Troodon*, was created in 2001.

1948
Elmer and Elsie, autonomous machines that mimic human behavior, are created.

1961
The first industrial robot is developed at General Motors car factory.

1969
First electrical-powered robot arm is made by Stanford University.

1970
Shakey is the first mobile robot created that "plans" its actions and solves problems.

1997
The robotic Mars Pathfinder rover roams on Mars.

2015
ASIMO, Honda's advanced robot, is programmed to run, jump, walk, talk, and solve problems.

2015
Humanoid robot Han can recognize and interpret human facial expressions.

BUILDING BOTS

IT ALL LOOKS SO SIMPLE IN
THE MOVIES: THERE'S A BIG ROBOT-OPERATED
factory that churns out hundreds of humanoid robots a day. Well, maybe in the future, but most of today's robots are created the old-fashioned way—by humans.

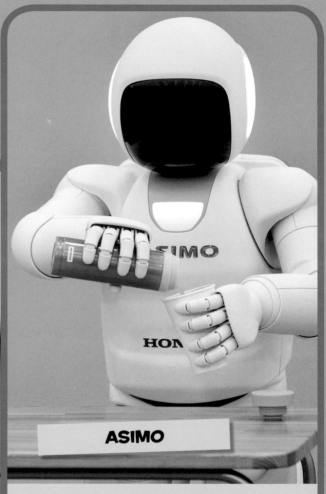

ASIMO

WINGED DRONE

Roboticist and micro air vehicle (MAV) team leader Dr. Gregory Parker holds a small winged drone that resembles an insect. Lightweight drones like this will have many uses.

ROBOT BUILDERS

Constructing a robot is a lot of hard work and can take years. The ASIMO robot took almost 30 years to create, and roboticists on the project had to have knowledge not just of robotics, but of mathematics, physics, and human anatomy as well. Through many trials and errors, ASIMO's creators made more than 11 working prototypes before coming up with the current version of ASIMO.

BOT BITS SPOT, A ROBOT DOG, WEIGHS 160 POUNDS (73 KG)—ABOUT THE SAME AS A GREAT DANE.

JUST LIKE ROVER

Sit. Lie down. Fetch. Most dogs can perform these common commands. But what about a robot dog? Can it do them, too? Yes, but not as easily as you might think. A real dog has bones, tendons, and muscles that help it move. A robot dog has steel bones, cables and springs for tendons, and an actuator such as an electric motor or hydraulics to provide "muscle" power. A robot dog also has a power source such as a battery, a pump, or a compressor (for large robot dogs). The power source supplies energy to keep it running, and an electric circuit and computer controls tell it where to go and what to do. To create a robot dog, robotics engineers spend hours learning the anatomy, or structure and function, of a real dog. They have to know the details of how a real dog moves, so they can program each movement a robot dog makes. BigDog, a 240-pound (110-kg) robot dog created for the U.S. military, has 50 sensors that measure height, speed, motion, and force. The sensors allow the robot to accurately determine how to walk on uneven terrain. Created in 2005, BigDog has been constantly tested and upgraded, with every movement studied so that small adjustments to its construction and programming can be made.

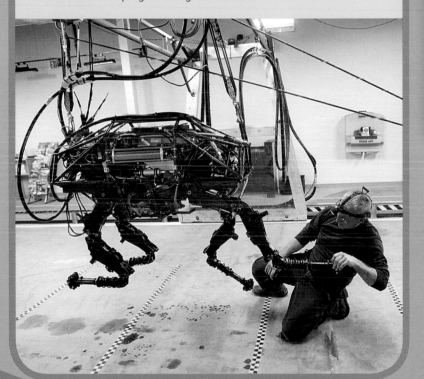

IN THE **1400s**,
ARTIST AND INVENTOR
LEONARDO DA VINCI
MADE A **MECHANICAL HORSE**
AUTOMATON AND DREW UP PLANS FOR A
ROBOT KNIGHT TO RIDE IT.

ROBOT—FROM CONCEPT TO COMPLETION

Ever wanted to build a robot but didn't know where to start? Check out this five-step process to get your bot-building in gear.

1. **WHAT IS YOUR ROBOT'S PURPOSE?** What will it do? Will it walk, talk, see things, have moving arms? Deciding on what your robot will do will help you figure out the next part.

2. **GATHER MATERIALS.** Once you know what type of robot you will build, go out and get your supplies. Find a place to create your robot and get things ready.

3. **BUILD YOUR BOT.** Start putting the pieces together. First the body, then the wheels, arms, legs, brain, etc. Don't forget the motor. This bot needs power!

4. **PROGRAM IT!** This is probably the most important part. You need to tell your robot what you want it to do.

5. **TEST IT OUT.** Give it a command and let it go. If you've done everything correctly, your robot will respond. If not, well, then you do what all good engineers do: You check all your steps and try it again.

By the Numbers

2 inches (5 cm) per second is the maximum speed the robotic Mars Opportunity rover attains while roaming Mars.

4 Robonauts have been developed by NASA.

10 million Roomba robot vacuums have been roaming floors and sucking up dirt and dust since 2002.

26 joints were used to fit together ASIMO's body parts.

178,132 manufacturing robots were purchased in 2013.

ROBOT SENSES

THE FIVE SENSES:

SIGHT, SOUND, TOUCH, TASTE, AND smell. It's how we humans interact with the world. Our brain uses these senses to help us make sense of the world around us. When we lose one of those senses, the others come to the rescue. They become stronger to help make up for the loss. But what if you are a robot? Robots don't have real eyes or noses. How do they get information from the world around them? Simple. A computer program tells them. Programming technology is becoming so advanced that robots are beginning to have the same keen senses as humans.

EXPLORER'S CORNER

Robotic technology uses sensors to learn more about the world. This has completely changed science and conservation. Robotic sensors can measure important information faster and more accurately than many scientists and park rangers. My work includes building systems that can react and notify me when they measure increased pollution in water. They can also listen for gunshots from poachers in protected reserves, and even watch to see if fishing boats are fishing in places they aren't allowed to go. These technologies are currently being used to protect whales in the ocean and to help protect elephants in Africa.

SNIFFER BOTS

Robots are being used to help sniff out dangerous gases, fires, and even bombs. Sending a robot in to sniff out and find a bomb is much safer than sending a human. Of course, the best noses belong to animals. And the silk moth may be just the animal to give robots the edge on sniffing. Scientists have put male moths inside a robot, attached them to a trackball, and had them track a female moth via her smell. As the male moth moved, the trackball rolled across sensors in the robot and recorded the smells coming off the female moth at that moment. The result was amazing. The robot learned to track smells as it followed the female. This robotic technology could be very useful in tracking the sources of environmental spills.

Shrewbot is a robot equipped with touch-sensitive feelers designed to mimic those of a shrew—a small mole-like animal with poor vision. Shrewbot can sense its surroundings without relying on visual cues. This makes it ideal to use in dark and confined spaces and for search-and-rescue missions.

SHREWBOT

34.9 °C

21.0

iCub has a funny-looking head, but the bot can "see" and "hear." iCub also has amazing grasping and moving abilities.

LASER EYES

Did you know that your body gives off heat? That is one way by which a robot can "see" you. It reads your thermal signature, or the heat your body gives off. Some robots also have infrared laser sensors that they use to see you. The sensors sort you through heat, color, and distance. This tells the robots your size, shape, and location. It also allows them to steer around you without running into you.

iit
ISTITUTO ITALIANO
DI TECNOLOGIA

iCUB

S/N: 000

BOT BITS JAPANESE ROBOTICISTS HAVE DEVELOPED A ROBOT CALLED PEPPER THAT CAN SENSE HUMAN EMOTIONS.

CYBORGS AND HUMANOIDS

SO, WHAT'S THE NEXT STEP IN

ROBOTIC TECHNOLOGY? IS IT CYBORGS—THE MACHINE hybrids of science fiction? Or is it a merging of robotics and medicine to create devices that replace lost limbs or help paralyzed people to walk again?

BIONIC HAND

HELLO, CYBORG!

A cyborg is a human with an enhanced ability to do something because of a mechanical implant or device. So that means that anyone who uses an electronic health device, such as a hearing aid, a pacemaker, or even a prosthetic leg, could be considered a type of cyborg. How cool is that?

ROBOTIC EXOSKELETONS

Imagine being paralyzed and using a robotic exoskeleton to walk again. It sounds out of this world, but it is part of the ever expanding world of rehabilitative robotics. These devices, including pneumatic muscle actuators (PMAs), work like powered human exoskeletons and muscles supporting the body much like an insect's exoskeleton does. They can be attached to a human body like a bionic suit. They allow some people in wheelchairs to walk, and others to use arms and hands that have been badly injured in accidents or war.

BOT BITS   ROBOT ANIMALS INCLUDE A ROBO-ANT, A ROBO-COCKROACH, AND EVEN A ROBO-JELLYFISH.

HUMANOID ROBOTS

Come on. Admit it. Sometimes you like to look at yourself in the mirror, don't you? Well, what if you could make a robot that looked and acted just like you? Cool? Or creepy? Scientists have learned that people are fascinated by machines that look like them. So, they have responded. The iCub (a robot that looks like a three-year-old child) and Topio (a robot that looks like a tall man) are just two of the many humanoid robots that have been created. These robots not only look like humans—they can do a lot of the same things humans can. iCub has all of the senses of a human child and is able to learn through interaction with its environment. Topio has long arms and is a champion Ping-Pong player. He also does chores around the house.

ANIMATRONICS

Animatronic machines are lifelike puppets that are electromechanically operated. Like humanoid robots, they are designed to look realistic and often imitate animal or human characteristics. But animatronics are more like remote-controlled toys than robots. Their movements are determined by an operator, often called a puppeteer, using a remote-control system. Animatronic machines are often used in the film industry. One well-known animatronic film animal was the 20-foot (6.1-m)-tall *Tyrannosaurus rex* that was a "star" in the Jurassic Park movies.

29

A PHOTO GALLERY

ROBOTS AROUND US

A patient uses a robotic SaeboFlex device during physical therapy. The glove helps him open his hand and grasp objects.

A technician makes an adjustment to the FACE humanoid robot. The robot was made to mimic human emotions in its facial movements.

Robotic surveillance flies could one day buzz around and report suspicious activity.

A humanoid robot greets guests and checks them into their rooms at the Henn-na Hotel in Nagasaki, Japan.

RI-MAN is a prototype robot being developed in Japan to help nurses lift patients into their beds.

Which one is human? Can you tell the difference? Danish professor Henrik Schärfe drinks coffee with his look-alike android robot, Geminoid-DK. The android is controlled by a remote operator and a computer. It can mimic Schärfe's body movements and facial expressions.

3
ROBO-HELPERS

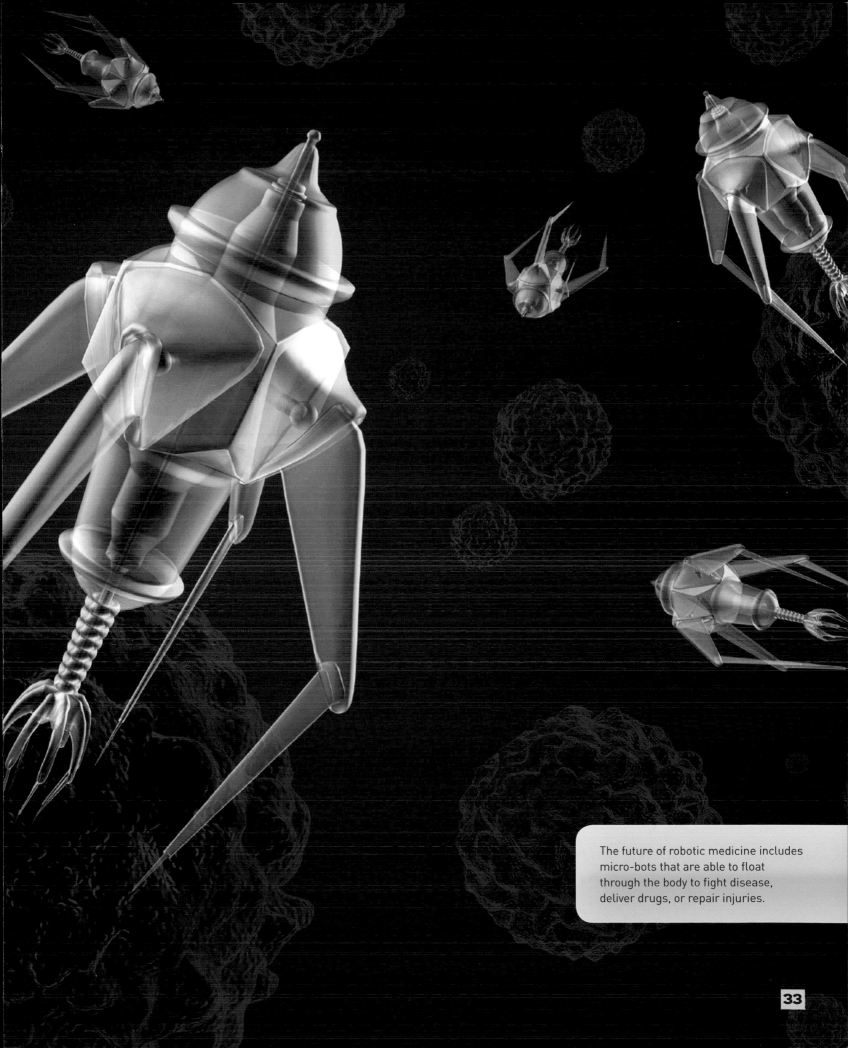

The future of robotic medicine includes micro-bots that are able to float through the body to fight disease, deliver drugs, or repair injuries.

IN THE HOME

CLEAN YOUR ROOM. SWEEP THE FLOOR. MOW THE LAWN. RAISE YOUR HAND IF YOU

like to do these things. Well, no one really does. And if robot makers have their way, you may not have to do them anymore. Home robots are becoming all the rage these days. They vacuum, iron shirts, wash your floors, entertain you, and can even bring you a drink.

ROBO-BUTLER, IRON MY SHIRTS!

Ever been at a hotel and need to get more towels? Or maybe you forgot your toothbrush. Never fear, Botlr is here. The 3-foot (0.9-m)-tall robot butler has made its debut at an Aloft hotel in Southern California, U.S.A. It rolls down hallways, searching 40 feet (12.2 m) in front of itself for obstacles, and can even go on elevators by itself. When Botlr is needed, the hotel staff simply enter in the room number, and Botlr navigates itself to the proper room. It can hold toiletries, towels, and even a newspaper. Eventually, updated Botlr models may be able to deliver room service to hotel guests, too.

HERB (Home Exploring Robot Butler) is a robotic butler designed to help people. It is known for its ability to separate a sandwich cookie with its sensitive robot hands.

HERB

HERB

Carnegie Mellon University

BOT BITS BOTLR USES WI-FI/4G TO COMMUNICATE WITH THE ELEVATORS AND "PUSH" THE BUTTONS.

34 NGK EVERYTHING

SWEEP NO MORE

Tired of cleaning your floors? Don't worry. The iRobot company has created a fleet of high-tech robot surface cleaners that live to sweep, mop, and scrub. With the push of a button, the Roomba zooms across carpet and wood floors vacuuming anything in its path. Need to mop? No worries, there's a robot for that, too! The Braava will mop your floor, and the Scooba will scrub dirt or grime buildup. Oh, and don't forget to lift your feet as the Roomba zooms past. The sensors help it navigate around objects, but why risk it?

ROBO-BUDDY

Feeling lonely? Look no farther than Pepper the robot. Designed to be the perfect companion, Pepper will sit and talk to you, respond to your questions, and even sense your mood. He's like a walking, talking mood ring. Pepper is programmed to respond to your emotions and interact with you like a real person. Pepper was designed to be like a real "live" friend—except his battery lasts only 14 hours before he has to be recharged.

This robot toy makes a purrfect pet.

CONSTRUCTO-BOTS

Robotic arms assemble vehicles in an automotive plant.

CHANCES ARE, THE
CAR OR BUS YOU TAKE TO SCHOOL

was built with the help of a robot. Most of the packaged foods you eat, from bottled juice to chocolates, are packed and dispensed by robots. Robots can weld, paint, assemble tiny pieces, lift, stack, sort, and even inspect finished packages before they are distributed. Industrial and manufacturing robots can do a lot of the same tasks that a human can, but they do it faster and more efficiently.

ROBOTIC CO-WORKERS

In many car plants, human workers work alongside robotic arms, assembling car seats and doors. A robotic arm is able to move on six different axes, or directions, just like a human arm. The antigravity springs on either side of the arm also allow it to pick up heavy items and move them around over and over again for hundreds of vehicles a day. In a car plant, robotic arms lift and fit heavy parts, such as door panels and windshields, and place them on a car body. Human workers then swoop in and assemble smaller parts. Some car companies are also outfitting their human assembly-line workers with robot tools such as wearable exoskeleton arms. These arms hold the weight of the workers' arms and make it easier and less tiring to perform repetitive work such as turning screws and cranking with tools.

BOT BITS ROBOTS AT A TIANJIN AUTOMOTIVE PLANT IN CHINA CAN WELD AN SUV IN 86 SECONDS.

WELDING

PACKING

LABORATORY

ROBOTS REPLACING HUMANS?

In many areas of manufacturing, robots have long replaced humans. They do the difficult, repetitive, fast, and fiddly automated work. They assemble whole, or parts of, automobiles in automotive plants. Food manufacturer robots can sort foods according to size faster than their human counterparts. Unlike most home robots, however, the manufacturing robots don't look like humans. They may only have one powerful industrial arm—or two arms attached to a base. They also stay in one place and usually do just one job.

ROBOT SWARMS

Eek, it's a robot swarm! Luckily, this swarm isn't something that will sting you. Scientists at Harvard University have created these swarms of tiny robots. They hope the swarms may one day help clean up oil spills, go on deep-sea adventures, and even explore far-off planets. The tiny robots, some no bigger than the size of a penny and some the size of a toy car, are designed to behave like animals that swarm, such as ants, bees, and termites. The swarming robots receive a programming signal all at once. It tells them where to go. The robots head out in one group, and move together, but do not have a collective intelligence. That means there is not an overall brain controlling them. Right now they can only form letters and numbers, but future applications look promising.

Robot swarms grouping together.

FAR-OUT BOTS

WISH YOU COULD GO WHERE NO HUMAN HAS

GONE BEFORE? THERE'S A GOOD CHANCE THAT A ROBOT HAS ALREADY

been there. Robots have traveled to planets that are far, far away. They have trekked across uncharted and uninhabited worlds. Robots dive deep in the ocean and reach depths no human could ever dream of going—all in the name of research.

MARS ROVER

ACROSS THE RED PLANET

Curious about life on Mars? You're not the only one. Scientists and engineers at the National Aeronautics and Space Administration (NASA) want to know, too. They have been sending robotic probes and rovers to the red planet for decades. The Curiosity rover is basically an intergalactic traveling laboratory. It is responsible for recording the climate and temperature of Mars, and it even drills, scoops, and analyzes the content of soil samples. The traveling robot is about the size of a small car and comes equipped with 17 different cameras to record every aspect of the red planet. The rover's long humanoid arm can pick up things, and even dig in the rocky soil. It has six wheels, each with its own motor, which allows it to maneuver up and down mountains and into and out of craters. The Mars rover relays its information back to Earth via the Deep Space Network of antennas.

NASA has sent several Mars rover robots to explore the planet.

BOT BITS THE ROSETTA SPACECRAFT TRAVELED IN SPACE FOR TEN YEARS BEFORE LANDING ITS PHILAE RESEARCH ROBOT.

UNDER THE SEA

Deep in the world's oceans, in areas too difficult for humans to venture to, robots are exploring the ocean floor. Remote-controlled diving robots can dive deeper in the ocean than any human can. They give scientists information about plant life, animal life, and the geographic conditions of the ocean bottom. Remote-controlled diving bots are tethered to a cable connecting them to their command modules, or ships on the ocean's surface.

Autonomous underwater vehicles, or AUVs, are robots that are completely tether free. They are programmed to dive up to 6,000 feet (1,829 m) deep and to gather information about the environment there. That's five times the height of the Empire State Building without needing to be connected to humans at the surface.

DIVING ROBOT

PHILAE LANDER

The robotic Philae probe landed on the surface of a comet in 2014. Its solar panels lost battery power and shut off, but regained power months later and started working again.

ROBO-ASTRONAUT

ROBO-ASTRONAUT

Robonaut, created by NASA, is a robot astronaut that helps out on the International Space Station (ISS). Robonaut's fingers are almost as flexible as those on a human hand, which means they can grip, turn, screw, and even climb around the ISS by holding on to handrails. Robonaut 2 (R2) has been equipped with legs so it can go on space walks by itself.

CANADARM

The remote-controlled Canadarm can repair satellites and space equipment.

TO THE RESCUE!

ROBOTS ARE TACKLING
SOME OF THE MOST DANGEROUS
and tricky jobs around, including fighting fires, sniffing for bombs, performing surgery, and diffusing hostage situations.

Doctors operate remotely with robotic equipment.

DR. ROBOT

Robots are assisting doctors in surgery, too. The da Vinci system, named for the famous inventor, can help doctors perform precise procedures through tiny incisions. The system uses 3-D imaging to see inside the patient, then mimics the movement of the doctor's hands. Since the system's "fingers" are more compact than a human's, the incision is much smaller, which means faster recovery time.

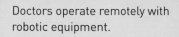

EXPLORER'S CORNER

Some of the greatest successes we have had in conservation technology have come from the use of drones to protect some of Africa's most iconic wildlife, namely the rhinoceros. Populations of rhinos have dwindled to near-extinction levels as a result of poachers seeking out their horns which sell for a lot of money on illegal markets. Conservationists have begun to use drones, sensors, and supercomputers to catch poachers before they kill. Just knowing these robotic flying machines are watching has started to deter poachers.

OH, NURSE!

In Japan, they are developing robotic care workers for nursing homes as well as robotic devices that make it easier for human workers to lift patients. In North America, General Electric is working on a robot that will help surgical nurses sort, sterilize, and prepare tools for the operating room.

This nursing home worker wears a Hybrid Assistive Limb (HAL) suit that helps her lift patients.

BOT BITS PACKBOT BOMB DETECTION AND DISPOSAL ROBOTS WERE USED IN THE WARS IN IRAQ AND AFGHANISTAN.

FIREFIGHTER

Meet SAFFiR (Shipboard Autonomous Firefighting Robot), the U.S. Navy's newest firefighting robot. It is designed to keep sailors safe on their ships. SAFFiR uses its sensors to sniff out fires and participate in damage control procedures. It can display a 3-D map of the fire, operate a fire hose, and even "see" through smoke with its visual sensors. The humanoid robot can do all this while keeping its balance on two feet even through rough weather and rocky seas.

SUSPICIOUS PACKAGE ALERT

See a suspicious package? Never fear. PackBot is here. The long, multidirectional arm can reach out and pick up the package. Its camera gives a real-time, accurate picture to the human operator who is a safe distance away. PackBot is able to roll through up to 3 feet (0.9 m) of water. It is small enough to be folded into a backpack but also tough enough to roll across a minefield or to help soldiers search buildings for dangerous criminals.

PackBot does the dangerous work to "sniff out" bombs.

RISE OF THE DRONES

Flying robots ruling the skies? Well, not quite. But robotic drones, or unmanned aerial vehicles (UAVs) are used by the military, police, fire departments, and many others. Drones can be either remotely controlled by humans or autonomous aircraft programmed to fly a specific route. Some police departments are experimenting with using drones for breaking up riots. The compact flying machines are equipped with cameras to give police a real-time look at what's going on. The drones can even produce a loud boom to alert people to their presence.

UAVs may soon be a common sight in our skies.

SAFFiR is a firefighting robot used by the U.S. Navy.

ROBOTIC COMPARISONS

MACHINE VS. HUMAN

AS ROBOTS ARE GRADUALLY BEING PROGRAMMED to act and think like humans, it makes you wonder where humans end and robots begin. After all, robots have been programmed with five senses. But how do robots really compare to humans? Can they do everything we can do?

CHECK OUT THOSE MOVES!

You may be able to pop and krump, but that robot hip-hop B-boy isn't fooling anyone. Dancing is one feat that robots have not yet mastered. Humans can move in many ways and in multiple directions. Even the most advanced robots still seem a little stiff when they are moving, compared to a human. The Japanese dancing humanoid, Manoi AT01, can spin and do "the robot" but can't quite keep the beat as smoothly or playfully as its human counterparts.

HIGH FIVE

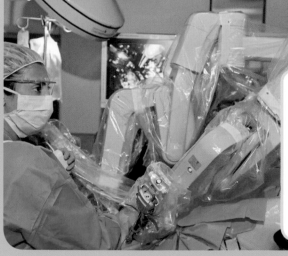

A human arm has a hand, forearm, elbow, upper arm, and shoulder. So do some robots. The human elbow allows the arm to swing 180 degrees. The da Vinci robotic surgery system can actually rotate 360 degrees, or a full circle.

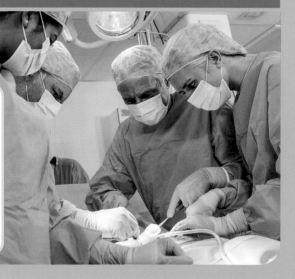

MOWING THE LAWN

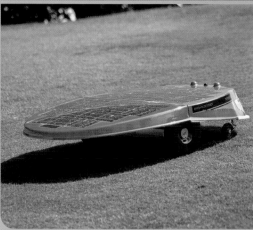

Grass cutting is an underrated skill for humans. For robots, it takes knowledge of the area to be cut and a lot of programming. Now enter the robot mower. This autonomous robot slices and dices the lawn on its own. But there is one problem: Current robot mowers can only work for about ten minutes before they have to be recharged again, which can take hours. You also have to embed wires at the edge of your grass so the mower knows where to stop.

THE EYES HAVE IT!

One of our greatest senses is vision. When your eyes see an object, that image is immediately sent to your brain. There's a whole portion of your brain that does nothing but interpret what you see. In fact, vision accounts for two-thirds of your brain's electrical activity. How can a robot compete with that? Robots with vision sensors use multiple video cameras that take images from several different angles and put all the information together. The computer processes the information, just like your brain does, then tells the robot what it is "seeing."

ENERGIZE ME

All humans need to eat to live. Food, especially nutritious food such as fruits, vegetables, grains, and proteins, gives us energy to think and move. Robots don't need to eat food, but they do need power to operate. Most use battery power. This NAO humanoid robot provides bank customers in Tokyo, Japan, with information on bank services. NAO sits while its batteries are recharged through a wall plug.

Robotics researchers pit their teams of robots against each other in a robot soccer world cup, or RoboCup, preliminary competition. The goal of the competition is to gain scientific knowledge and improve robot function.

4
FUN WITH ROBOTS

MADE FOR THE MOVIES

WHO DOESN'T LOVE A GOOD ROBOT SHOW?
MOVIES AND TELEVISION SHOW US ROBOTS IN ALL FORMS AND FOR

all functions. There's something about a robot that tugs at our emotions and makes us feel, well, more human. See if you can match these descriptions to the robots.

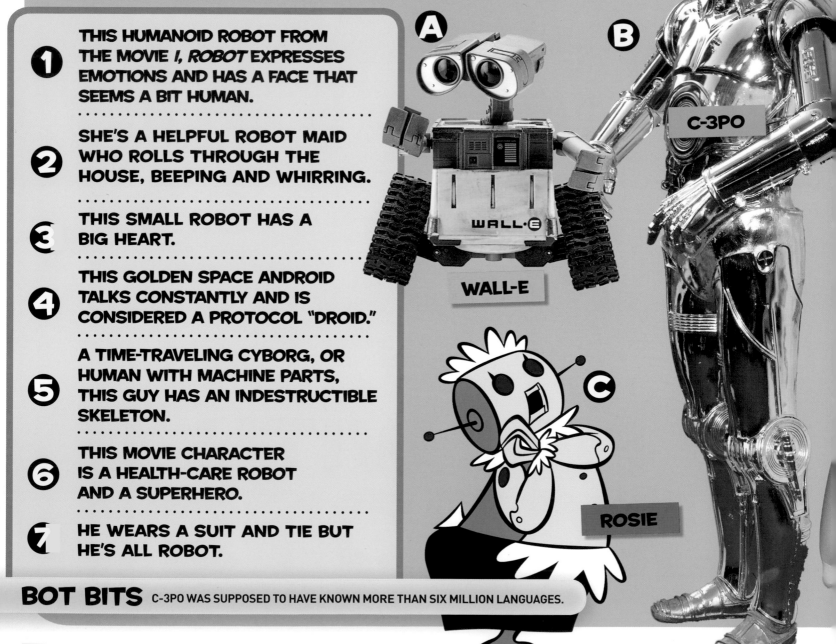

1 THIS HUMANOID ROBOT FROM THE MOVIE *I, ROBOT* EXPRESSES EMOTIONS AND HAS A FACE THAT SEEMS A BIT HUMAN.

2 SHE'S A HELPFUL ROBOT MAID WHO ROLLS THROUGH THE HOUSE, BEEPING AND WHIRRING.

3 THIS SMALL ROBOT HAS A BIG HEART.

4 THIS GOLDEN SPACE ANDROID TALKS CONSTANTLY AND IS CONSIDERED A PROTOCOL "DROID."

5 A TIME-TRAVELING CYBORG, OR HUMAN WITH MACHINE PARTS, THIS GUY HAS AN INDESTRUCTIBLE SKELETON.

6 THIS MOVIE CHARACTER IS A HEALTH-CARE ROBOT AND A SUPERHERO.

7 HE WEARS A SUIT AND TIE BUT HE'S ALL ROBOT.

A WALL-E

B C-3PO

C ROSIE

BOT BITS C-3PO WAS SUPPOSED TO HAVE KNOWN MORE THAN SIX MILLION LANGUAGES.

ANSWERS: 1. F; 2. C; 3. A; 4. B; 5. E; 6. G; 7. D

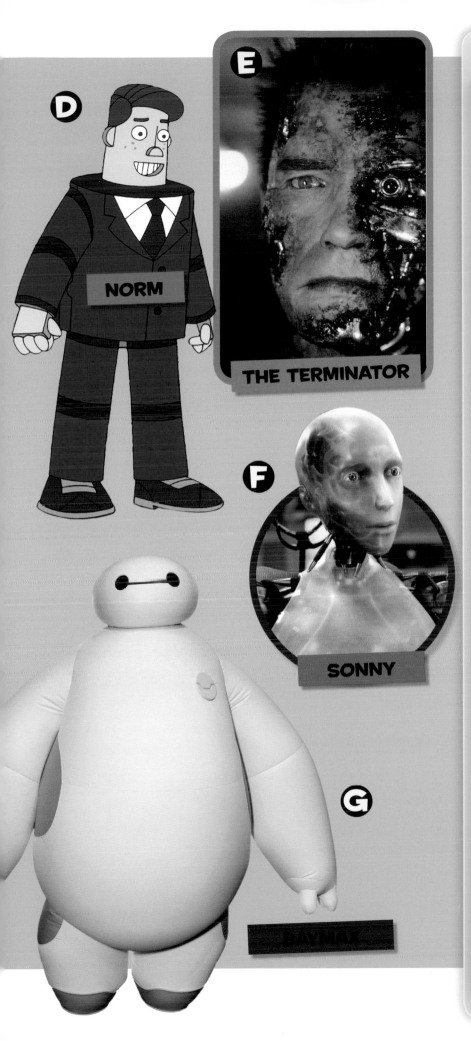

D

NORM

E

THE TERMINATOR

F

SONNY

G

BAYMAX

ANDROID FRIEND

Real-life robot scientists say Lt. Commander Data, from *Star Trek: The Next Generation,* is the most recognizable humanoid robot. Of course, Data is a fictional character played by an actor. But he is portrayed as a self-aware robot. Here are some of Data's special abilities and characteristics:

POSITRONIC BRAIN—It functions as a central processing unit and allows Data to make quick calculations.

SUPERIOR ANDROID STRENGTH AND ENDURANCE—Data can overpower humans and other robots. He can also survive in environments that humans can't, such as in space and underwater.

PASTY FACE—Data does not appear too lifelike.

NO EMOTIONS—Data cannot "feel" pain or pleasure like humans, but in later episodes he does have an "emotion chip" installed to allow him to replicate human emotions.

IMMUNE TO DISEASE—As a machine, Data cannot get sick, but he can suffer from computer viruses and energy malfunctions.

OFF SWITCH—Data can be turned off by a button located between his shoulder blades.

LT. COMMANDER DATA

ROBOTICS CHALLENGE

DO YOU HAVE WHAT IT TAKES TO BE A

NATIONAL GEOGRAPHIC EXPLORER? CAN YOU DESIGN, BUILD, AND TEST

a plan of action the way a scientist or robotics engineer would? Thousands of kids around the world took up our Engineering Exploration Challenge to solve real-world problems that explorers face in the field.

ANIMAL MIGRATIONS

Some animals are on the move—yearly, seasonally, and some even daily! Explorers want to know more.

YOUR CHALLENGE:

Design, build, and test a way to study a migrating animal using your own robot-like design. Your solution must help scientists better understand your animal's migration.

TELLING THE STORY

There are special places on Earth that need our protection.

YOUR CHALLENGE:

Design, build, and test a way to collect real data about a place, either close to you or far away, using your own robot-like design. Your solution must tell the story of why the place you've chosen is special.

EXTREME ENVIRONMENTS

Some places on Earth are extremely awesome. But how do you study them when they're dangerous, far away, or difficult to get to?

YOUR CHALLENGE:

Design, build, and test a way to study an extreme place that you'd like to explore but cannot go to because of extreme conditions, using your own robot-like design. Your solution must be able to collect data and send it back to you.

PROBLEM SOLVED!

Participants in National Geographic's Engineering Exploration Challenge were asked to solve challenges that explorers face when researching. The challenges included designing a robot that could study animal migrations, collect information and tell a story about a place, or explore extreme places and environments. Our budding explorers, ages 6 to 18, came up with inventive solutions for robots that could collect information about their environment and take action based on that information. Check out some of the solutions!

OCEAN EXPLORER

BURLINGTON, NEW JERSEY, U.S.A.:

"For the Extreme Environments Challenge, I designed the aye-aye robot ocean explorer. The aye-aye is my favorite animal at the zoo. It is nocturnal. My robot works at night and sleeps in the day, so it is nocturnal, too. Its antennas make it float to the top of the ocean to get solar energy. They are like balloons. When it is dark outside, the sea-bot sinks down. It can walk on the bottom of the ocean with its feet. One eye takes pictures and one eye takes videos. Aye-aye sounds like eye-eye! It has bright orange antennas to help the scientists find it when it floats to the top. It looks like a crab, so sea animals try to be its friend and the sea-bot can take pictures of its friends up close. I think the aye-aye sea-bot will help people know more about the ocean, and the Earth has a lot of ocean."

—Marcy, age 7

An illustration of the aye-aye sea-bot.

Aye-Aye Sea-Bot

Video

Camera

FOLLOW THE HUMMINGBIRD

DEERFIELD, ILLINOIS, U.S.A.:

"Our solution to the Animal Migrations Challenge was to create a drone capable of following a hummingbird on its migration. To do this we would put a GPS chip on the hummingbird's leg. This GPS would transmit its location to a GPS chip on the drone. The drone could then follow the hummingbird on its journey, staying within 15 to 35 feet (4.6–10.6 m) of the hummingbird so as to not disturb it. Our drone would have a camera that would take pictures of the hummingbird every time it stops for more than five seconds. It would also have a thermometer that would take the temperature every 12 hours, so it could measure the temperature difference at its starting and finishing point and the places in between. So it can last the long trip, the drone will be battery powered and gasoline powered. When the drone is going slow enough, or is stopped completely, the batteries will recharge themselves."

—Team Lightbulb, age 11

Team Lightbulb

A detailed drawing of the group's hummingbird migration challenge specs.

YOU CAN PARTICIPATE, TOO!

Check out the challenges, choose one, and start your engineering engines. Go to **NatGeoEd.org/NGX** for more details.

ENGINEERING EXPLORATION CHALLENGE

BLEEP, BLOP, BLOOP!

JUST LIKE HUMANS, ROBOTS HAVE THEIR
OWN LANGUAGES, TERMS, AND TITLES. AND LIKE HUMANS, ROBOTS
are named, but robot names usually reflect their purpose, skills, or parts.

Agile Justin was designed as a space-bot but can perform just as well on Earth. It is stable and has agile arms and hands. Justin is also called Rollin' Justin because of its wheels.

ROBOT NAME GENERATOR

You got your name from your parents. But where does a robot get its name? From the people who created it! Roboticists usually determine a robot name from one of these four ideas: its function, parts, the type of robot it is, or a "human name." Sometimes, robot names are acronyms, or abbreviations of initial letters of words used to make up the name, such as Protection Ensemble Test Mannequin, or PETMAN. Use these steps to determine your own robot's name.

1. WHAT WILL YOUR ROBOT DO? WILL IT HAVE A SPECIFIC JOB?

2. WHAT TYPE OF PARTS DOES THE ROBOT HAVE? SOME ROBOTS HAVE NAMES WITH ENDINGS LIKE -OID, -BOT, -TRON, -ATOR.

3. WHAT TYPE OF ROBOT IS IT? DOES IT RESEMBLE A HUMAN, OR AN UNDISGUISED PIECE OF MACHINERY?

4. HOW ABOUT A NICKNAME INSTEAD? WOULD A SIMPLE HUMAN NAME MAKE IT MORE ACCEPTED AMONG YOUR FRIENDS AND FAMILY?

If your robot is a cleaner bot designed specifically to tidy your bedroom for you, you could name it for its purpose: Fast Acting BedRoom Cleaner, or FABRC, for short.

If it is an android that keeps you company and cleans your room, you could call it Spiffy, so that your family and friends see it as an easygoing cleaning buddy.

If your robot is simply a mechanized arm on wheels that is programmed to clean your room, you could call it the Dust-a-nator.

AGILE JUSTIN

BOT BITS KITT, the robotic car from *Knight Rider*, a 1980s TV show, was short for Knight Industries Two Thousand.

BUILD A ROBOTIC BEE

Your mission? Pollinate a field of crops and return to the hive! Your method? Build your own bee! Use the sensors, power supply, and end effectors illustrated here to build a robotic bee. Make sure that it has the correct balance of power, weight, and sensor capability to return to the hive. Remember, the more gadgets you add, the more power you need! But the bigger the power supply, the heavier your bee will be. Choose carefully!

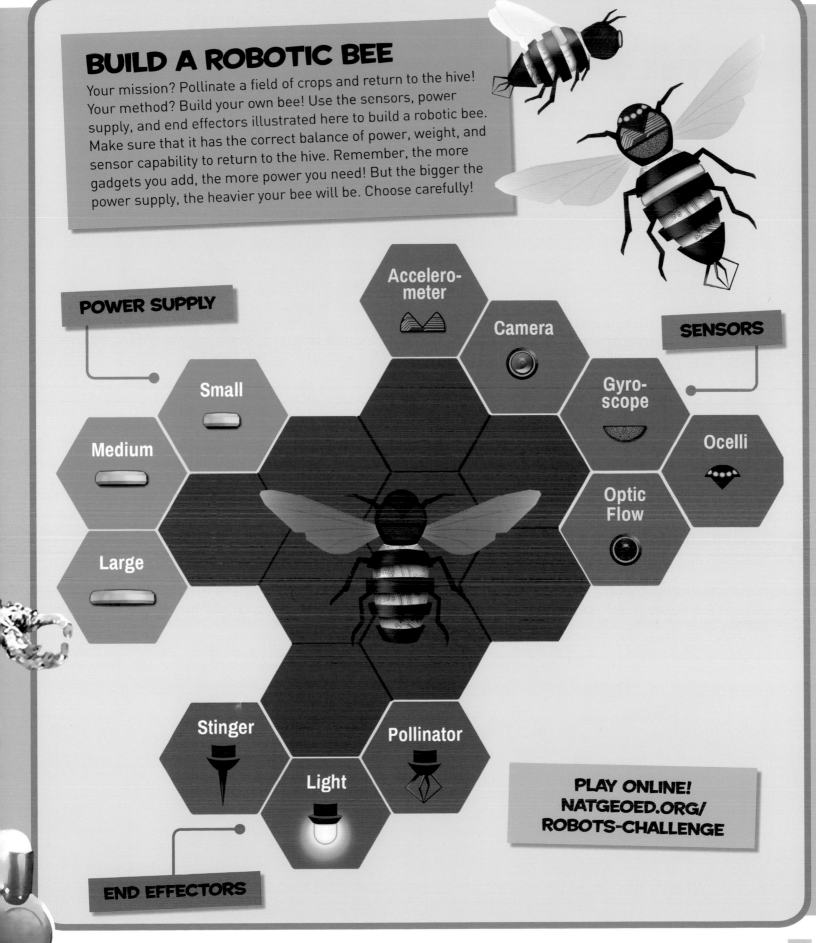

POWER SUPPLY

Small

Medium

Large

Accelero-meter

Camera

SENSORS

Gyro-scope

Ocelli

Optic Flow

Stinger

Light

Pollinator

END EFFECTORS

**PLAY ONLINE!
NATGEOED.ORG/
ROBOTS-CHALLENGE**

MYTH VS. FACT

MANY PEOPLE THINK

THEY KNOW WHAT THE FUTURE HOLDS for humans and robots. Some people fear a day when machines rule the Earth. Others say that fear is unfounded. Can you guess which of these statements about robots are myth and which are fact?

A SCIENTISTS ARE WORKING TO CREATE A MAGGOT ROBOT THAT WILL SUCK OUT PARTS OF YOUR BRAIN.

B ROBOTS WILL PUT EVERYONE OUT OF A JOB.

C THE SMALLEST ROBOT IS SMALLER THAN A SPECK OF DUST.

D AUTONOMOUS ROBOTS ARE VERY SLOW.

E ROBOTS WANT TO TAKE OVER OUR WORLD.

B. MYTH

Almost every company that uses robots does so because they want to improve efficiency. Humans will always be needed to program, manage, and make decisions for robots. Robots are useful in that they can do the boring jobs and difficult jobs that require heavy lifting, but they are also limited by what their programs contain. That means changing a process, even slightly, requires much more work when robots are involved.

A. FACT

Researchers are designing a maggot robot to find tumors in the brain. Remotely controlled by a brain surgeon, the maggot robot is meant to be tiny and flexible so that it can move inside your brain without harming it. Researchers hope that the robot maggot will one day be used by surgeons to burn and suck up cancerous tumor tissue.

BOT BITS A NANOBOT CAN BE 100 TIMES SMALLER THAN ONE HUMAN RED BLOOD CELL.

C. FACT

Scientists are working on microscopic robots called nanobots, nanomachines, or nanomites. These miniscule robots are so small that they work on molecules. They can act together like a swarm of bees, or independently by swimming through your bloodstream to deliver medicine to a particular cancer cell. Researchers hope to use medical nanobots injected into the human body to fight disease.

D. FACT

Autonomous robots are very slow. It takes a lot of programming for a robot to act independently. All that programming takes time to process. Take for example, PR2, the home robot. An engineer successfully programmed it to fold a bath towel, but it took 25 minutes for PR2 to get the job done. And when faced with an entire basket of towels, it only folded them correctly 50 percent of the time.

E. MYTH

This idea, while found often in books and movies, is just not true. At this time, robots can only do one or two things really well, if they are programmed to do them. They are not capable of thinking totally independently. They are programmed to look for certain things and to perform certain tasks. Although some robots may have sensors that allow them to "feel" their environment, they do not completely understand it.

PHOTO FINISH

BEHIND THE SHOT WITH SHAH SELBE

ONCE IN A WHILE, YOU FIND
A PLACE ON THIS PLANET THAT IS TRULY SPECIAL

and unique. Botswana's Okavango Delta, in sub-Saharan Africa, is one of those places. This wetland river delta doesn't flow into a lake or sea, but directly into the middle of the Kalahari Desert. That makes it a critical habitat for some of Africa's best known wildlife, such as elephants, hippopotamuses, rhinoceroses, lions, leopards, hyenas, and more. I work as the lead engineer for the Okavango Wilderness Project, which aims to protect the delta and share it with the world for years to come. We do that through a yearly expedition on dugout canoes, and by installing my technologies in key areas.

Much of the conservation technology we use relies on robotic innovations to help focus our eyes and ears on this amazing place. There are certain things that robots can do that are too dangerous or repetitive for humans to do efficiently. For example, we fly drones high overhead to help us count wildlife and plot a safe path for the expedition as we travel. These flying robots help us to send up pictures and video that we can use to assess wildlife populations, check the health of plant life, and determine the flows and levels of the water. We also use underwater robots, also called remotely operated vehicles (ROVs), to explore the channels and to areas underneath the papyrus. The robots help us to see below the surface of the water because it is far too dangerous for people to do that with all of the hippos and crocodiles around. We also install microcontroller sensors throughout the delta that can tell us if there are any threats to the environment. These systems can measure the water or air, determine if there are any pollutants or risks, and send a notification to us before it is too late.

Our sensors are so easy to build and program, that with a little know-how, many of you reading this could replicate it and do the same conservation technology work we do in Africa. We are turning this ecosystem into a connected environment that will allow us to protect it in ways that were never possible before robotics. This technology will improve life on this planet in ways that we never expected!

Project researchers made the trek through the remote Okavango Delta in dugout canoes.

National Geographic Explorer Shah Selbe works on the robotic drones used in the Okavango Wilderness Project.

AFTERWORD

THE EVOLVING WORLD OF ROBOTICS

SO THAT'S ALL THERE IS TO
KNOW ABOUT ROBOTICS AND ROBOTS. OR IS IT?

The field of robotics is just beginning to take off. Scientists and engineers continue to work toward the goal of creating robots that can help humanity. They want robots and robotic parts for all areas of our lives: medicine, work, school, the military, the home, and even in space. We will have robots that can go to galaxies we've never been to, so that we can peek at new planets and solar systems and try to understand the secrets of the universe. Medical researchers are working to create nanobots that can be put inside a person to destroy diseases such as cancer, or to stimulate a brain when it misfires. Robots will keep us safe by policing our streets and keeping traffic lights steady. Robots may soon be our caregivers, helping us when we are sick and unable to take care of ourselves. Perhaps they will even become our friends. With the advances in emotion sensing, that is certainly a possibility.

For some, though, the real question is where do we draw the line? Is there a point where robots will go from being helpful to wanting to take over the world like they do in the movies? That is highly unlikely. At the present time, robots are not intelligent enough to think independently. They must be programmed to think, and they have to access many different sensors to understand the world around them.

The robotics field is in constant need of young people who are interested in robots and engineering. If that describes you, get involved! Find a robotics club near you. If there isn't one, start one. Learn all you can about how robots work. Maybe even design and build a robot on your own. You are never too young to create a robot. In 2010, 14-year-old Easton LaChappelle made a robotic arm using Legos. In 2013, he used it as a model to create a prosthetic arm for a girl who was born without one.

Or, feel free to sit back and let the robots vacuum your floors, mow your lawn, and fold your laundry. After all, robots are here to help!

In the movie *Chappie,* a police robot prototype is programmed to think and feel like a human. Chappie can make independent decisions to kill or help humans.

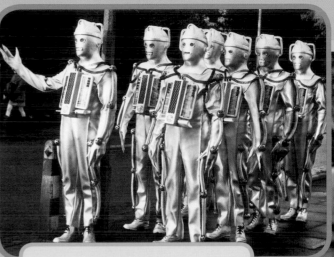

In the TV series *Doctor Who*, Cybermen are emotionless machines that are part human and part robot. They want to destroy humans.

Robot waiters deliver meals to customers at a robot-themed restaurant in China. The robots take customers' orders, then deliver them by following a magnetic track from the kitchen to the tables.

AN INTERACTIVE GLOSSARY

ROBO WORDS

Research shows humans feel more comfortable with robots that look and act more like humans than machines. Here, designers have given a robot human facial structures such as eyes and teeth.

CAN YOU TALK LIKE A ROBOTICIST? GIVE THESE

robot words a try! Read through this list of words and meanings to test your robotics knowledge and vocabulary. Then check out the page numbers listed to see the words used in context. The answers are listed at the bottom of this page.

1. Animatronics

The use of electronics to make robots move like real-life people or animals.
(PAGE 29)

An animatronic dog makes a great pet because it can:

a. bark

b. dig

c. jump

d. all of the above

2. Artificial Intelligence

The ability of a machine to make decisions and show intelligent human behavior
(PAGES 18, 20, 23)

What traits does a robot with artificial intelligence have?

a. a strong body

b. independent thinking and reasoning skills

c. the ability to listen

d. the ability to speak

3. Autonomous

Describing something that can act independently
(PAGES 10, 18, 23, 39, 41, 43, 52, 53)

What makes the Mars rover autonomous?

a. its ability to map the surface of Mars

b. its ability to analyze the images it sees

c. its skills at mapping out a safe route

d. all of the above

4. Cyborg

A part-human and part-machine hybrid
(PAGES 28, 46)

Which devices would make a person a cyborg?

a. a pair of eyeglasses

b. a hearing aid

c. a prosthetic limb

d. a contact lens

5. Drone

An unmanned craft that can navigate independently
(PAGES 16, 17, 24, 40, 41, 49, 54, 55)

What can drones do?

a. fly around without a human pilot

b. steer a ship

c. sail a boat

d. drive a car

6. Exoskeleton

A hard outer structure that provides support for an animal's body or a robotic device
(PAGES 28, 36)

Exoskeletons are found on:

a. dogs

b. robots

c. insects

d. both b and c

7. Humanoid

A robot that looks like a human
(PAGES 12, 13, 15, 17, 18, 22, 23, 24, 29, 30, 31, 38, 41, 42, 43, 46, 47)

Which of these is a humanoid robot?

a. HERB

b. ASIMO

c. AlphaDog

d. Dante II

8. Microcontroller

A tiny microcomputer with its own operating system
(PAGES 11, 54)

What can microcontrollers do?

a. power computers

b. make milkshakes

c. destroy robots

d. process information, and store and run programs

9. Nanobot

A very tiny robots the size of a nanometer
(PAGES 13, 53, 56)

What do scientists hope to do with nanobots in the future?

a. fight wars

b. explore space

c. fight diseases such as cancer

d. power computers

10. Roboticist

A scientist who designs, builds, programs, and experiments with robotics
(PAGES 7, 10, 24, 27, 50)

What do you need to study to become a roboticist?

a. engineering and computer science

b. biology and design

c. engineering and geography

d. medicine and computers

11. Sensor

A device that detects and measures things in the environment such as light or sound
(PAGES 11, 17, 19, 25, 26, 27, 35, 40, 41, 43, 51, 54, 56)

What do robots use infrared laser sensors for?

a. to "smell" you

b. to "see" you

c. to measure speed

d. to determine the temperature

12. Swarm

A bunch of tiny robots all acting together, like insects, as a giant group
(PAGES 37, 53)

What do scientists someday hope robot swarms will do?

a. follow insects

b. make other robots

c. cure diseases

d. clean up oil spills or explore space

ANSWERS: 1. d; **2.** b; **3.** d; **4.** b and c; **5.** a; **6.** d; **7.** b; **8.** d; **9.** c; **10.** a; **11.** b; **12.** d

FIND OUT MORE

Be on top of technology with these websites, books, movies, and places to visit.

MOVIES

Kids: Ask your parents for permission to watch.

Star Wars: A New Hope
Lucasfilm/Disney, 1977

WALL- E
Disney-Pixar, 2008

ROBOTS 3D
National Geographic
movies.nationalgeographic.com/movies/robots/

National Geographic's *ROBOTS 3D* documentary shows how fast robot technology is moving. *ROBOTS 3D* features a number of humanoid robots, including iCub, PR2, and HERB the Butler, and is a fascinating and fun look at how robots are changing the world.

PLACES TO VISIT

Carnegie Science Center
Pittsburgh, Pennsylvania, U.S.A.

MIT Museum
Cambridge, Massachusetts, U.S.A.

Museum of Science and Industry
Chicago, Illinois, U.S.A.

National Museum of Emerging Science and Innovation
Tokyo, Japan

BOOKS

How Robots Work
Jenny Moss
Capstone, 2013

Recycled Robots: 10 Robot Projects
Robert Malone
Workman Publishing, 2012

The Robotics Club: Teaming Up to Build Robots
Therese Shea
Rosen Publishing, 2011

WEBSITES

Kids: Ask your parents for permission to search online.

NatGeoEd.org/NGX
Every year, the National Geographic Engineering Exploration Challenge gives young people ages 6–18 the opportunity to design, build, and test solutions to engineering challenges.

asimo.honda.com
This site gives you the inside information on the ASIMO robot, billed as the world's most advanced humanoid robot.

robonaut.jsc.nasa.gov
Learn what robonauts do and watch videos of NASA's robonauts preparing for space flight.

www.robothalloffame.org
The hall of fame website was started in 2003 to recognize major achievements in robotics. You can read about them here.

thetech.org/exhibits/online/robotics/
The Tech Museum website has a section with a robotics time line, activities, and information on how robots work.

Acknowledgments: Special thanks to Dan Ipema, P. Eng., and Wendy Scavuzzo

NG Staff for This Book
Shelby Alinsky, *Project Editor*
James Hiscott, *Art Director*
Jeff Heimsath, *Photo Editor*
Debbie Gibbons, *Director of Intracompany Cartography*
Paige Towler, *Editorial Assistant*
Sanjida Rashid and Rachel Kenny, *Design Production Assistants*
Tammi Colleary-Loach, *Rights Clearance Manager*
Michael Cassady and Mari Robinson, *Rights Clearance Specialists*
Grace Hill, *Managing Editor*
Alix Inchausti, *Production Editor*
Lewis R. Bassford, *Production Manager*
Rachel Faulise, *Manager, Production Services*
Susan Borke, *Legal and Business Affairs*
Neal Edwards, *Imaging*

Published by the National Geographic Society
Gary E. Knell, *President and CEO*
John M. Fahey, *Chairman of the Board*
Melina Gerosa Bellows, *Chief Education Officer*
Declan Moore, *Chief Media Officer*
Hector Sierra, *Senior Vice President and General Manager, Book Division*

Senior Management Team, Kids Publishing and Media
Nancy Laties Feresten, *Senior Vice President*
Erica Green, *Vice President, Editorial Director, Kids Books*
Jennifer Emmett, *Vice President, Content*
Eva Absher-Schantz, *Vice President, Visual Identity*
Rachel Buchholz, *Editor and Vice President,* NG Kids *magazine*
Jay Sumner, *Photo Director*
Amanda Larsen, *Design Director, Kids Books*
Hannah August, *Marketing Director*
R. Gary Colbert, *Production Director*

Digital
Laura Goetzel, *Manager*
Sara Zeglin, *Senior Producer*
Bianca Bowman, *Assistant Producer*
Natalie Jones, *Senior Product Manager*

Editorial, Design, and Production by Plan B Book Packagers

Captions
Cover: Toyota's Partner Robots are capable of the complex movements needed to play the drums, violin, and even the trumpet!
Page 1: The Meccanoid G15 K robot toy responds to voice commands and is programmed with over 1,000 phrases.
Page 2–3: A robot awaits adjustments in a robotics laboratory.

For more information, please visit nationalgeographic.com, call 1-800-NGS LINE (647-5463), or write to the following address:
National Geographic Society
1145 17th Street N.W.
Washington, D.C. 20036-4688 U.S.A.

Visit us online at nationalgeographic.com/books

For librarians and teachers: ngchildrensbooks.org

More for kids from National Geographic:
kids.nationalgeographic.com

For information about special discounts for bulk purchases, please contact National Geographic Books Special Sales: ngspecsales@ngs.org

For rights or permissions inquiries, please contact National Geographic Books Subsidiary Rights: ngbookrights@ngs.org

Library of Congress Cataloging-in-Publication data

Swanson, Jennifer, author.
  National geographic kids. Everything robotics : all the photos, facts, and fun to make you race for robots / by Jennifer Swanson.
      pages cm. — (National geographic kids. Everything)
  Audience: Ages 8-12
  Includes bibliographical references and index.
  ISBN 978-1-4263-2331-7 (pbk. : alk. paper) — ISBN 978-1-4263-2332-4 (library binding)
  1. Robots—Juvenile literature. 2. Robotics—Juvenile literature. I. National Geographic Society (U.S.) II. Title. III. Title: Everything robotics. IV. Series: Everything series (Washington, D.C.)
  TJ211.2.S93 2016
  629.8'92--dc23
                                        2015019559

Printed in Hong Kong
15/THK/1